# KEEP GOING
# No Matter What

## The Reginald F. Lewis Legacy: 20 Years Later

*Produced by* LOIDA NICOLAS LEWIS
*Interviews by* PONCHITTA PIERCE

BOOKMARK PUBLISHING CORP.
New York, NY

**Bookmark Publishing Corp.**
115 East 57th Street
Suite 1430
New York, NY 10022
212-756-8946

ISBN-13: 978-0-9886318-1-6

Library of Congress Control Number: 2012955699



Coordinated by Linda Langton • www.bookmarketinginternational.com
Designed by Gary A. Rosenberg • www.thebookcouple.com
Edited by Elliott A. Wiley • www.rejassociates.com

Printed in the United States of America

*This book is dedicated to the legacy of my beloved husband, Reginald F. Lewis, on the 20th Anniversary of his transition to eternal life.*

*He left us too soon.*

# Contents

FOREWORD

# Kenneth I. Chenault

When I was a young man, Reginald Lewis came to the Black Law Students Association at Harvard to talk about his alma mater, his early days as a lawyer and the decision to start his own firm. He was intense. He was focused. His entrepreneurial spirit was inspiring. It was clear that we were hearing from a man who was going to make a difference in the world around him.

Even to a first year law student, it was apparent that Reggie was not a man to let barriers get in the way. He had big ideas and he was going to make them a reality—in the legal profession and in the world of business.

When Reggie set his sights on leveraged buyouts, it wasn't long before he completed his first successful deal for the McCall Pattern Company in 1984. He broke new ground a few years later when he orchestrated—what at the time was the largest off-shore leveraged buyout—the $985 million purchase of Beatrice International Foods.

As head of the most significant black-owned business in the nation, he paved the way for a generation of African American business leaders who followed. His combination of business excellence and personal achievement set a standard that withstands the passage of time.

I had the good fortune to know Reggie, not just as an outstanding entrepreneur, but as a man who cared deeply about giving back to the community and helping others succeed.

Reggie left us twenty years ago at the young age of fifty, but his legacy endures at places like The Lewis International Law Center at Harvard, which he established to help train the legal profession's next generation of leaders.

It also endures through the work of his wonderful wife and partner, Loida. Her leadership at the Reginald F. Lewis Foundation makes possible initiatives such as the Reginald F. Lewis Museum of Maryland African American History and Culture. The Museum, which collects, preserves, interprets, documents and exhibits the rich history of Maryland's African Americans, is located in Baltimore where Lewis was born and grew up.

Reginald Lewis had a favorite saying that underscored his approach to life and business. It has inspired many of the people who contributed to this book: "Keep going no matter what."

*Kenneth I. Chenault*
*Chairman and CEO*
*American Express Company*

INTRODUCTION

# Loida Nicolas Lewis

It hardly seems like twenty years since the passing of my husband, Reginald F. Lewis. In many ways he is still a constant presence.

We met when, after I had been sworn in as a lawyer in the Philippines, I was in New York as part of a world tour with my sister Imelda Nicolas. Reginald's Harvard Law classmate, Reynaldo Glover, suggested that I meet Reg as a blind date. This was the beginning of a wonderful twenty-five-year relationship, which only ended with his death after a brief illness on January 19, 1993.

God is good in that I was given the gift of meeting Reginald and of becoming his wife, lover, friend and mother to our two daughters, Leslie and Christina. The things that impressed me most about him were his vision, ambition, integrity and tenacity. Most of all, he was a family man who enjoyed the simple joys of extended family reunions and camaraderie.

The world took notice of my beloved when he engineered the nearly $1 billion leveraged buyout of Beatrice International Foods in 1987.

When he died, among the things Reginald left unfinished, that I took on, was the book of his life he was writing about. He titled it, *"Why should white guys have all the fun?"*

Together with Rene "Butch" Meily, the company's Public Relations executive, we engaged journalist Blair Walker to finish the book and then to have it published by John Wiley & Sons. In 1994, *"Why should white guys have all the fun?" How Reginald Lewis Created a Billion-Dollar Business Empire"* was published and made the best-seller list in *Business Week*. Since that time, many men and women who read *"Why should white guys have all the fun?"* have been inspired to "reach for the stars" so to speak.

In addition, the Reginald F. Lewis Foundation that my husband started in 1987 continues his tradition by helping people, with emphasis on supporting educational and cultural institutions.

In this book, *Keep Going No Matter What—The Reginald F. Lewis Legacy: 20 Years Later*, some of the people inspired by my husband share their thoughts and insights into how Reginald F Lewis, or his book, impacted their lives and what they have learned from him.

Ponchitta Pierce has listened to these observations and written them for this book, which also includes comments from the leaders of some of the institutions that have been supported by the Foundation.

In all things, may God be glorified!

Loida Nicolas Lewis
Thanksgiving Day, 2012, New York City

*PHOTO CREDIT: Frank Hoefsmit*

# Michael "Mike" Muse

*MICHAEL "MIKE" MUSE is Co-Founder and CEO of Detroit-based Muse Recordings, an independent record label; a hip-hop radio and TV personality; producer of a Broadway play; and guest commentator on the business of music, pop culture, and politics at highly rated urban radio stations and colleges around the country.*

I joined Kappa Alpha Psi Fraternity at the University of Michigan. We fraternity brothers were always recounting stories of notable Kappas and Reginald Lewis's name always came up. One thing Reginald taught was very transferrable skills. He was a lawyer, yet he went on to become owner and CEO of a multinational food company through the most brilliant leveraged buyout of our time. I don't think anything in law school can prepare you for that. I started out as an engineer doing nuclear chemical research. Now I'm running a successful music record label.

I remember reading the book, *All You Need to Know About the Music Business*, and I thought, "Oh, this is easy, anybody can do that." I had visions of what it would be like, the mission statement, the business statement, how I would differentiate myself from the rest of the other independent record labels out there. Let me tell you, I got told "no" quite often. But just as Reginald did, I went back to the drawing board and kept re-tweaking. I had the unbelievable tenacity to find a yes behind every no. That's what Reginald did. I wasn't afraid to fail and to say how can I make this better, to get to a point where we can get a yes or no, and finally Muse Recordings happened. Reginald Lewis was a huge model in terms of benchmarking what life could be. No one could put you in a box and that was brilliant.

Although you are a financial genius, it's not about attitude, but about having access to capital, to the right people who can validate you within these circles. It doesn't matter what your GPA was coming out of college. It's who do you know that can get you into the rooms to meet these partners that will make people comfortable doing business with you, especially if you're an unknown African American. At the time that Reginald was coming up, which makes the story that much more brilliant, was the fact that here's an unknown African American male who is entering essentially a world that is controlled by white men. With an unknown track record, not only did he prove himself, he was able to enter into this world and have great success and be one of the greats at it.

It's the same thing within the music industry. You can be the most creative genius in the whole wide world; however, if you don't have access to those who have positions to say yes to your records, to radio play, to partnerships, to advertising campaigns, that means your product won't get heard. There are so many great musicians out there right now who don't even have the ability to get their music out. There are no outlets provided to them. They don't have the resources or access to them. It all comes down to finding that yes within every no. Those are the ones who win. But it comes from that unbelievable drive that Reginald had, to keep fighting at all costs, to keep pushing forward.

I'm with three unknown producers who have never produced a Broadway play before and we have this goal in mind of making the Richard Pryor story a reality on Broadway. And we're fighting tooth and nail to make it happen. It's going to take some finessing, hard work, blood, sweat and tears, which we're going through right now. But who's to tell us we can't do it? With every no, I just get more inspired to find a yes, which gives me the incredible drive to do it.

I was having lunch with a mentee, a recent graduate of a high school in New York City that represents some underserved populations. As part of his graduation gift I gave him the Reginald Lewis book because it just shows a young person there is no barrier to you. It's not about your starting point. It's about how you finish. You may be dealt a hand that may not be the best of cards to play. But the point is, you do have a card somewhere that you can play within your deck and you've got to use it the best way you can.

# Mellody Hobson

*MELLODY HOBSON is Chairwoman of DreamWorks Animation SKG, Inc., and President of Chicago-based Ariel Investments—which manages more than $43 billion in assets—and Chairwoman of Mutual Funds. Ariel is reportedly among the largest American-owned money management and mutual fund companies in the United States.*

The surprise was that Reginald Lewis could make it happen, find that level of funding and execute the transaction as flawlessly as he did. I got a sense he was all consumed with his work and that ultimately he was going to be the guy who died with his boots on.

I don't know how to make the train go faster in achieving what he did. But I think it's inevitable, although it's going to be a while. In some situations it's racism, but I think people are pretty well intentioned. They don't even understand the biases that they have. Reverend Jesse Jackson calls it cultural blinders because people just don't have the perspective to understand that they're exclusionary. They have to be told it is unacceptable.

There are plenty of qualified people who could be the CFOs of many Wall Street companies. Our sights are already set there. It's just a function of making sure we're getting an equal opportunity to participate. We have different people, obviously Oprah and others, but not the way he did it in financial services. That is ultimately probably one of the most important industries there is. He surprised people with his achievements because he was a pioneer, and when you're a first and only, it's surprising and inspiring.

Just because you're good doesn't mean you'll be discovered and become great. You've got to push hard and relentlessly. Your ideas have to be like a beacon. The quality of the service or product that you plan to offer has to be the driving force behind your passion and energy.

My mother has said to me since I was old enough to walk, "Birds of a feather flock together." You want to surround yourself with talented and smart people at all times. You don't want to be the smartest person in the room. You want to have people to take you to new heights.

Our community has also been extraordinarily interested in creating wealth and maximizing opportunities for itself. We don't learn about investing in school in the United States and we don't grow up in homes where the stock market is generally discussed. This puts us behind the eight ball. 401K plans have put investing front and center in our lives and we're selecting mutual funds and the like for our retirement. So that at least opens the dialogue and people who invest in 401K plans also invest outside of them.

We also have an Ariel Community Academy Arts School, which has a savings and investment curriculum where we give every first-grade class $20,000—real dollars—to invest. The money follows them through their grade school career as they take over increasing responsibility for managing the money. We're socializing black kids about the importance of investments.

I didn't grow up in the world of finance, but my mother strongly believed in education. I was obsessed with school. With six children in our family, I used to do my homework in the bathroom because it was the only quiet room in the house. I would run the tub water to drown out the noise.

People in our community, when they see me doing financial reports on television, for example on ABC's *Good Morning America,* will tell me they didn't know people like me existed. There were no black women talking about financial investing before I started doing it about twelve years ago. Role models are very important in life. There's a saying, "You can't be what you can't see."

# Mario Baeza

*MARIO BAEZA, a former partner at Debevoise Plimpton, is currently head of Baeza Group, an investment company specializing in the Pan-Hispanic region. He helped launch V-me, the first Spanish-language public broadcasting network. He is also a music writer.*

I heard Reginald Lewis speak at Harvard. He was so commanding in his presence and clear in his vision on how law, politics, power, and economics all play together. He became an inspiration for me. Lewis helped open my eyes to certain things that I later pursued in the practice of law. Of course he went on to do great things at Beatrice. He had the Drexel guys behind him and they have a way of figuring those things out. I thought that he was playing with the team that could win. He had a very good shot and he pulled it off. It was an amazing thing to see at the time. It was such a huge transaction and, for us, really became a beacon of what's possible. Wow! Here was a minority person who was able to use the system in a way that we got a big piece of the pie. That hadn't been done before. I don't know that anyone's ever done it since.

There was a window, and that's how life is. These windows of opportunity historically open up for very short periods of time. It's a constant struggle to keep them open. You have to have not only the preparation, which Lewis had, but also the nose to see the opportunity and not fool around with that. The stars lined up, he saw the time was good, had the right kind of connections and partners that he cultivated and he made it happen.

When Reginald Lewis did his extraordinary transaction, there were an awful lot of black mayors. They, all of a sudden, looked at the majority firms who were doing all of the municipal bond work, which is very easy and lucrative and said, "How come there are no minorities?" Lots of them had maintained bond deals and relationships for a hundred years, with all-white teams and no diversity. And the mayors, literally overnight, said, "No, we're not doing that." When Wall Street was flush, everyone lining their pockets up sufficiently, their conscience or politics got to them and they said, "We have to do something so that we look like we're more socially responsible."

So there was a push for the big guys to line up with a minority-owned investment bank or asset manager, as in the case of Utendahl Capital or Raymond Blaylock and his company. They were saying, "Hey, you know, there's a lot of money being made in all these public offerings and underwritings. We can cut them in for a piece, it doesn't hurt us and it looks good to start fostering some diversity on Wall Street."

Now roll forward four to eight years and no black man is mayor of a major city. Do you think these firms show up with the minority partner? No! And these guys don't have business. Classically what happens is when there's a period of retrenchment, all things go out of the window and they're viewed as unnecessary excesses. If you haven't been able to consolidate your business and become independent from the people who helped you, you get pruned. The same thing about windows of opportunity is true for law firms. They go through this push for more black or Hispanic partners in the law firms. Today I'm aghast. You look thirty years later at law firms, and the amount of black or Hispanic partners in the ranks and the pipeline, it's probably gone backwards. If not, it's grown very, very little.

When I think about it, a major factor of minorities taking advantage of windows of opportunity was Jesse Jackson when he put together "The Wall Street Project." There was also the New American Alliance working to get Hispanics on corporate boards, scholarship programs for MBA students, corporate board trainings. Everybody on Wall Street was more or less terrorized because Jesse could make your life uncomfortable. If you're a CEO at Blackstone or Goldman Sachs and you get a call from Jesse Jackson at that time, it's like, this can't be a good thing when Jesse says, "I want to come see you."

# Samuel I. "Sandy" Rosenberg

*SAMUEL I. "SANDY" ROSENBERG, a lifetime Baltimorean, represents the 41st Legislative District in the Maryland House of Delegates and is Vice Chairman of the Ways and Means Committee. He studied political science and law and has known the Lewis and Fugett families since he met Reginald F. Lewis's younger brother, Jean S. Fugett, Jr., while both were students at Amherst College.*

We were in the same class, and both from Baltimore. I was the editor of the newspaper, *The Amherst Student*, in our junior or senior year and Jean was the number-two guy on the paper. Jean, a tight end, played football with the Dallas Cowboys and then the Washington Redskins. I would go to games with members of the family. When Jean played in Super Bowl X we all went together and, afterward, Reginald took us to dinner. I think that was the first time I met him. This was in the 1970s. Working on things like the buyout of a company was not something that I was interested in doing. While I wanted him to succeed, and I understood what was going on, I would not engage in a Socratic dialogue of what, where, if you do this, then why. The mainstream Baltimore press didn't give much attention to his exploits and accomplishments, perhaps because of his race, but also because he wasn't doing it in Baltimore.

Carolyn, the matriarch of the family, says I'm a member of the family. She worked at the post office, and Reginald's stepdad, Butch, was at the National Security Agency. I didn't know his dad, Clinton Lewis. Carolyn's been involved in the Baltimore Archdiocese, in leadership positions in the community. If she were in her son's generation she would have been a leader in business or public service, but in her day the post office was one of the few options available for African Americans. It's a very tight-knit family. Reginald's widow, Loida, is still very much a part of the family and appropriately so. Carolyn sees preserving her son's memory and his leadership role, through the Reginald F. Lewis Museum, as an important family responsibility. The original idea for an African American museum in downtown Baltimore as part of the Inner Harbor came from House Member Pete Rawlings, father of the current mayor, Stephanie Rawlings-Blake.

Reginald was a path breaker, a very bright guy, a lawyer and an entrepreneur as well. We would get into spirited discussions on issues because I would come, and still go, to family Thanksgiving and Christmas dinners at their homes. He would never talk shop, but we would engage in policy or sports discussions. He was a fierce debater and there were times when we disagreed on issues, but it didn't carry over to the dinner table.

Reginald was in business, but I love politics. I've been in the House of Delegates for thirty years. In the Maryland legislature, if you have a half-decent idea and know how the legislative process works and how to move your bill forward, you can get things accomplished. And that's a great fulfillment for me. I enjoy the process of learning about a problem, or how somebody else has tried to address it and then using the governmental process to make a positive change.

Being in politics requires different qualities than those of a CEO. It's not just what is best for your district or the people in the neighborhood. Ultimately you have to convince a lot of other people it's in the best interest of the state. When you're an entrepreneur, you're used to running the show and calling the shots. You may have to negotiate with the unions—I don't know if the businesses Reggie owned had unions. But if you're a good CEO, and used to saying "This is my best judgment," then you consult with people in your business. And once you've made a decision on what is best for your company, "Bam," you carry it out.

PHOTO CREDIT: *Maryland Government*

# Olive Haye

*OLIVE HAYE, a business major at Georgetown University, was motivated by Reginald Lewis's life of hard work, discipline, and determination. She wanted to follow in his footsteps and go into mergers and acquisitions. She had studied classical ballet for thirteen years, but decided she wanted to leave behind a legacy for future little black girls who never thought "financier" could be an option for them. Now twenty-one years old, she realizes Wall Street is not for her.*

Dancers only have a short time to work and their income doesn't really go much higher than minimum wage. With ballet I can literally see my results—my leg gets higher, my turns get tighter. It's just more visual and so much fun. After reading Mr. Lewis's book, and seeing how much financiers make and how they change the world, it seemed to me that Wall Street was a more advantageous career than ballet. He was struggling and grinding for the longest time. He didn't come from a financial or upper-echelon New York family. It just shows how hard work pays off. My ultimate goal was to break the mold, just as Mr. Lewis did. But I never realized how hard the work was.

Finance is also such a guy's world. It's the epitome of an old boy's club. It's going to be ten times harder for me to break the glass ceiling than it was for Mr. Lewis, a black man, because he was still a man. It's hard to communicate with a colleague on a strictly platonic level. When I started interning, it was so different, the way they look at you and talk to you, like a woman, not a colleague. My boyfriend goes and gets drinks with his coworkers but I can't do that because my coworkers are all males. I'm the only woman in the office and it's kind of awkward. There's this weird tension.

After-hours networking is much harder. It's a very thin line you have to walk as a woman. During the daytime it's fine. I'm trying to adjust my tone, and how I dress and how I walk, because you want to be feminine, but not sexy. You have to tiptoe around everything—your hair, your makeup, and your tone of voice. It can't be too girly, but it can't be too masculine. Men don't have to do that. For Mr. Lewis it might have been the same, but around race lines. You don't want to be a stereotypical black male. For me, it's making sure I'm not a stereotypical black woman—loud and everything, like what they might see on TV.

On Wall Street you really have to be cutthroat. You have to really depend on other people so much, whether or not they like you. In ballet it's all up to you. You just work hard and you'll succeed and be the prima ballerina if you're good enough. Human nature is to fight, crawl and kick other people down to get to the top. I don't think my moral code is going to allow me to be that successful in finance. I'm not that ruthless.

Although I changed my thoughts about Wall Street, I learned a lot from Mr. Lewis's book. One was the importance of being prepared. Even if you are behind the curve, there is always a way to get on the same level as your competitors. Opportunities mean nothing if you are not prepared.

Networking is also important. I learned to always ask questions 24/7 and to probe everyone I knew who could help in advancing my skill sets. If I'm on the trading floor and confused, I don't shy away from asking a broker to explain something. If there's anything I don't know, I make sure to find out.

My dad ingrained in me to be the best. I knew if I was excellent, I would be successful. Mr. Lewis instilled in me that "You cannot break the rules without knowing the rules."

# Kenneth I. Chenault

*KENNETH I. CHENAULT is Chairman and CEO of the American Express Company and one of the first African Americans to become the CEO of a Fortune 500 firm.*

Reginald Lewis was a good competitor. Anything you read about Reggie, or certainly people that you talk to, will tell you that whether it was on the athletic field, or in business, or academically, Reggie had an incredible will to win. I think you've got to have courage because, the reality is, to be a winner in anything you have to take some risks. You have to work hard and have an unshakeable belief in yourself. You wouldn't be human if you didn't waver, if you did not have self-doubt. And I'm sure Reggie had moments of it, but what's critical—and this is where character comes in—is that you overcome that self-doubt and you persevere.

You could look at sports for an example. Reggie and I both played sports in school. The importance here is, if you want to be good you have to work hard at your craft. Secondly, you understand there are things that happen that are outside of your control. Third, anyone who is engaged in sports has had some adversity and some failure and you have to overcome that—whether it's the experience of losing a game that you really wanted to win or that you're injured and you're not able to play. You have to overcome that injury and come back to experience the exhilaration of winning again. And if you can do that, both as an individual competitor and as a member of a team, those are experiences you can transfer into business. In my career and in my job I've had to think big, to be a visionary, to develop leaders and, fortunately, I have had some success in bringing about transformation in our company. Reggie was really a terrific role model, a pioneer who broke new ground and someone who really opened the doors for a lot of people.

What I think you've got to focus on if you want to win is your performance. That's what is critical for any successful person. I think that was personified in Reggie, because he really did not let obstacles prevent him from achieving his goals. That is one of the most important lessons Reggie left us with. When you go out on your own, from an entrepreneurial standpoint, you're going to have some failures. What is important is how you overcome these failures and keep focused and don't allow yourself to be distracted. Reggie didn't allow himself to be defined by any of his failures, and had the courage and creativity and optimism and confidence to push forward. Those are values that are instilled in you by your parents, teachers, friends as well as experiences that you had in school or on the job. With some people it's innate. For others, I really do think you can acquire these skills and attributes. At the end of the day, you have to have a positive attitude that you're doing something meaningful to be successful. That comes from your inner core and your belief in self.

We have seen an increase in the number of African Americans who own businesses. I also think it's particularly noteworthy that you have more African American CEOs of publicly-held companies, and what's important is that we have to succeed in a number of fields and categories. So we need more owners, more CEOs. Are you building the company from scratch or, as Reggie did, are you buying the company? It all comes down to the credibility and drive that you have. What's important is that he entered a field of leveraged buyouts, where he was the pioneer. And I think when you are the first it always makes a difference and increases the level of difficulty.

# G. "Jun" Delfin

*G. "JUN" DELFIN, born in the Philippines, moved first to Canada and then to the United States, where he has just become an American citizen. In 1994 he founded the insurance company, the Unlimited Agency, Inc. "America is a place where you can do what you want to do within the realm of legality and proper actions."*

I first learned about Reginald Lewis through *Business Week* magazine. After reading about him, I ordered his book, *"Why should white guys have all the fun?"* Everyone needs help in order to improve, and his book helped me a lot. He was so down to earth, yet at the same time a person of all angles in life in terms of economics, social issues, good politics and he was well rounded.

While my children were young, I started telling them about Mr. Lewis and showed them his book. The fact that he was an African American doing all of this at that time was very significant. I was intrigued with Mr. Lewis's sense of achievement and global leadership.

He had great success, but also setbacks and challenges. I believe in spiritual or intangible factors. They are just whatever the Supreme Intelligence or Supreme Creator instills in each of us. It's the quality of doing an extra-mile effort, always having this kind of perception that today is better than yesterday and tomorrow will be better than today. It's a belief in being an asset rather than a liability, being an instrument of the progress of civilization and having a conviction that nothing is impossible.

Each one of us is unique. I believe that in spite of the uniqueness, we are all interconnected. I also feel it's an inherent, insured right of a human being to maximize the instrument that has been given to us to fulfill whatever mission we have. There's no such thing as overnight success or achievement. It must be first within a person, and then it goes to the next level, the family. That family could be evolved into community and that evolves to the psyche at large.

I first met Reginald Lewis's wife, Loida, some eight years ago in the National Federation of Filipino American Associations. I'm glad that the culture I came from is the same as hers. I believe that a culture should be important. Each culture has its own good possibilities. That's where I view what justice and prosperity are all about in terms of the macro issues of life. Reginald Lewis could have lived in the Philippines, or any place in the world, because that was his God-given nature. The Lewis College, in Sorsogon City, one of the farming provinces in the Philippines, is named after him. Attorney Lewis said she named The Lewis College after her husband because he wanted to impart education to young people. For her, this was his way of paying back to the community. He respected everyone and, of course, in respecting everyone, he respected himself. And before loving everyone, he loved himself.

I came from two seminaries in the Philippines. I wanted to be a priest. When I met Mother Teresa, she asked me, "How come you are on the outside rather than the inside?" And I just answered, "Mother, I could serve Him even though I'm on the outside." Each of us has an intrinsic economic and market value. Additionally, we have an equally important factor—our future, which to me is equated to growth, change, and a never-ending quest for the sublime.

# Deborah C. Wright

*DEBORAH C. WRIGHT is Chairman and CEO of Carver Bancorp, Inc., the holding company for the Harlem-based Carver Federal Savings Bank, a federally chartered savings bank and the nation's largest African and Caribbean-American operated bank, with approximately $700 million in assets and 140 employees. Prior to joining Carver, Wright was President and CEO of the Upper Manhattan Empowerment Zone Development Corporation.*

I went to school with every intention of becoming a lawyer, probably in some kind of advocacy. Then I started reading about Reginald Lewis in *Black Enterprise* and hearing from older friends on Wall Street that he intended to be visible and that wealth was part of the picture. I was just happy to see somebody black doing well. I think I just took it as an article of faith that if he made it to those magazines, that something was going to come out of it.

Dealmakers are people who make quick decisions and enjoy the people part of making deals and the competitive part. There's the myth about him that he was sort of a self-made man, that he didn't need anyone and went through all this alone. I'm not close enough to the story to know the fact or fiction. It doesn't jive with what I know about people that I'm close to who are very successful.

Reginald Lewis was able to ignore conventional wisdom. He was certainly savvy enough to understand that what he was attempting to do was not easy and that it would come with a lot of struggle. The fact that he set the bar so high and just pushed to get there set an aspiration that none of us had ever dreamed of. He had an uncanny ability to leverage financial institutions for personal wealth, which is really important. The question then is how do you leverage personal wealth into community wealth?

I think about a wealth that endures as I walk the streets of Harlem, Bed-Stuy and Crown Heights, and I see the tremendous wealth that has slipped through our hands. I think about how we bridge that gap between an individual's success and community success. Once we get a hold on something of value, whether it's real estate or companies, we have to focus our energies around making sure that it lasts and that some of it is invested in people and in making smart business decisions like Reginald Lewis did. I'm all for the bright lights of individual success, and there was none brighter in my lifetime than Reg. The legacy to leave something behind—financial, cultural, and community institutions that will carry on the broader message of our past as a people—we have to do that, because at the end of the day if we don't do it, nobody will. It's what is required to create and perpetrate generational wealth. That's the way you make change.

We've lost the generation of people who saw the tremendous inequalities and things that were wrong. They lived to change that. What makes me so sad about the downside of their success and sending us off to these colleges is our thinking that Wall Street was the thing you had to do if you were smart and a competitive person. But look at what has happened to our people. Those of us who have been successful have moved out of our neighborhoods and left institutions like the Carvers. We forget that these institutions will wither away if we don't continue to stay invested in them. I think Reg would have said, "Why didn't black people rescue Carver?"

If Reginald Lewis had been a woman, none of his success would have happened. It's a sad reality. Human beings have not evolved that quickly. It's still a boy's club and some boys crossed the line and helped. I've been very fortunate to benefit from that. But it's not a broadly held practice as it should be. Nobody asks how important it was that he picked a smart wife. She could have grieved and taken care of her daughters and grandchildren and just kind of moved off the stage. She didn't choose to do that. Made of really great stuff, that woman. She's very quiet, but as strong as they come and smart.

# Sadiq Murray

*SADIQ MURRAY is currently President and CEO of the Onyx Organization LLC, located in Newark, New Jersey. Onyx operates as a parent company in areas such as residential real estate investment and development and small to mid-size acquisitions of private companies in various industries. Sadiq got his first taste of business at age nineteen when he formed an organization in his community with local kids "to find out how economics and politics work hand in hand."*

My children are young now but believe me. I'll give them a nice education about Reginald Lewis and other African American leaders. He was persistent and determined to overcome obstacles. I especially like his quote, "Because if you don't keep going, you never know what the outcome will be."

I can remember from the book, one day Reg was teaching his older daughter Leslie to ride a bike, and was pushing and pushing for her to keep going. Then he sat for a minute and suddenly it came to him, "Well, if I'm not ready, I'm not ready. And I have to get ready." And that's one of the things I've adopted. I have to form my own network, build relationships, and help people in whatever way I can, not just money, but personal time, and prepare myself for whatever is coming.

Whatever you're doing, just figure out a plan to do it and go after it. When you come across barriers, what you have to do is figure out exactly how to structure and attack the obstacle in such a way that you will be successful. Don't worry about the money. Don't worry about who's going to help you. If you don't start, it's not going to happen. You can't quit.

I also learned from him the value of starting small. You don't just jump straight to a level that you're not familiar with. You take steps towards your goal, and the overall objectives of the big picture emerge. Adopting not just his strategies, but also the way he went about moving toward his goals are the same things that I live by today.

Once you have a goal in front of you, you have to accomplish it. And it's never going to be in the time you think it's going to happen. You're going to have to go through a lot of bad apples before you get to the right one. You have to fight all twelve rounds. If you quit, that other fighter probably might have been willing to give up in that last round and you could have won. You can never just say, "You know what, I can't do it," because then you're not going to be successful.

I think Reginald Lewis made it more likely for African Americans to succeed in financial services today. The ones who know who he is and the ones who have their own individual goals, they were able to use his model to be successful. But for the individuals who did not know who he was, it's hard, because that was fifteen or so years ago and those young people just weren't in that industry or just weren't really knowledgeable about a lot of things.

Who knows what he would be if he were still alive. If he went public with Beatrice, he would definitely be a billionaire. He would be high on the *Forbes* list. He might have dabbled in politics around this time of his life, because he had a lot of integrity. His ability to get it done is the number one quality that you need to succeed as a politician. If he said he would do something, it got done. There's not an expiration date on it.

I think *"Why should white guys have all the fun?"* is a book that young kids should read in high school, especially if they're not sure of their career or what they want do. Once you read the book and find out a lot of the changes Reginald Lewis went through to get where he did, you might be interested in the investment community, entrepreneurship, philanthropy, non-profits or law.

Reg started his own law firm. You take a law student, or someone who's going to school who wants to be a lawyer, they might feel that, "Well, if he did it, I can have my own law firm, or start my own practice and be successful at it."

# Dan Gasby

*DAN GASBY, Chairman of B. Smith Enterprises Ltd., oversees day-to day operations of B. Smith restaurants. Dan started his career in television sales and moved to production, creating and producing "B. Smith With Style", a nationally syndicated weekly lifestyle program that aired nationwide and in forty countries. With his wife and partner Barbara Smith, they also created "B. Smith Style," the forerunner to "O" Magazine and the first national lifestyle magazine published by an African American woman.*

Reginald F. Lewis represented a time when it was trailblazing to be a successful businessman in the truest sense of the word. He understood law, business and was an entrepreneur. He cut a swath by himself. It wasn't like he had a roadmap of history in these businesses. Today you have second and third generations of people who are born into the business, but he wasn't. He was born into success. And that's from his mother and from what he learned through his own personal grit. One of the things that his mother said to him, that I've already said to my daughter, "Mean what you say, and say what you mean."

He wasn't a celebrity. There was no hip hop, no Russell Simmons, no P. Diddy or Jay-Z. He did it in business, negotiating, sitting across from some of the sharpest, shrewdest, toughest people in the world in a bare-knuckles, Wall Street, take-no-prisoners way. It's not how good you are. It's what did you do today and what are you going to do now that I can project and put value on. I think business people viewed him with fascination, awe, and envy.

Reginald F. Lewis couldn't get into the private club in the Hamptons in New York, but he was just as successful as anyone there, probably more successful. They were just in the lucky sperm pool. But when you get turned down, or when you've got to always prove yourself, or you're the one person that stands out, you can never miss a meeting because everybody knows that you're not there. So there's that tremendous amount of pressure. Not to mention your own internal pressures that drive you, but also the pressures your own people impose on you.

Being a black man in business is like—just imagine if I took my finger and tapped on your shoulder incessantly. Every time I'm tapping on your shoulder, or water is dropping on your head, it's Chinese water torture. It's the stress of always having to prove yourself. No one knows how much fight it took out of him just to get there, to have to run 150 yards to win a 100-yard race. He didn't get *carte blanche*. I can only speculate, but I'm sure he was always breaking new ground, having basically to go up against the unknown, always having to worry about being accepted. You look at the picture on "*Why should white guys have all the fun?*" and say, "If he were blond and blue-eyed with his brain, how much farther would he have gone? The doors would have opened quicker."

I keep his book by my bed because I look at his face and I know he looks like me. Nobody walks up to you and says, "You look like a banker." They may think you play ball or look athletic or maybe look like a lawyer, but they certainly don't say you look like an entrepreneur or think of you as a hedge fund guy. Especially back then, in the seventies and eighties. That was uncharted territory.

And Reginald Lewis says the most political things. Why should white guys have all the fun? Why should only they be in the country clubs? Be able to go to vineyards in France and Italy? It's so sad. It's what is missing in black America today. A large portion of our youth don't even know what fun is in terms of opportunities to grow and explore, be educated to different cultures and see how people can live in beautiful homes and travel. They're hitched to every kind of electronic personal device you can imagine. A lot of people today, if they see MLK they think it spells milk.

But what Reginald Lewis did was hard work. We don't want to take responsibility for raising our families, going to school, studying and not having fun on a Saturday night, apprenticing, or having mentors, and being gofers to learn the business or trade, to be the bottom man on the totem pole. He would be alarmed and disappointed that half of black men are not graduating from high school, which means that you're going to be poor for the rest of your life and not have opportunities.

I have an idea of where he came from, what East Baltimore was like back in the fifties and sixties. You cleaned your stoop and bought a Monte Carlo and listened to the Temptations and ate crabs in the back of the alley. Your goal in life was to work, get a job at age twenty-one for twenty years, get a pension at forty-two and then find another job. There's nothing wrong with that, but this guy had greater dreams and ambitions.

*I keep his book by my beside in Sag Harbor!*
*I will never achieve what he accomplished, but he laid a path for my progress.*
*What he achieved was remarkable; he was not an athletic hero or entertainer.*
*He made it through the tough scrum of business!*
*I thank him and will always salute him!*

# R. Donahue Peebles

*R. DONAHUE PEEBLES is Chairman and CEO of The Peebles Corporation, the largest African American owned real estate development firm in the United States, representing a high-end real estate empire stretching from Washington D.C. to Miami Beach to Las Vegas. Peebles details the secrets to his achievements in "The Peebles Principles."*

I started my company in the early 1980s when we were making the transition from Civil Rights to economic opportunity and empowerment. I grew up in Washington, D.C., which is a very political environment, without super entrepreneurs. There was a new class of entrepreneurs beginning to emerge and they were doing it on a government-contracting basis, on a much lower scale. I looked at other entrepreneurs, outside of that world, to get inspiration. There were the Donald Trumps, Mort Zuckermans, Trammell Crows, Gerald Hineses, the major national developers that were out there, but no African Americans. And then you looked across other business sectors—at the time, finance, mergers and acquisitions, and leveraged buyouts were getting a great deal of promise—people like Michael

Milken and others, and again, no diversity. Reginald Lewis represented African Americans competing at the highest levels in his profession, his industry—lifting barriers and trailblazing, and I was looking to accomplish a similar peak in the real estate development world. It's like basketball, playing your position. I'm well suited for entrepreneurship.

We're now the largest African American owned real estate development-company in the country. What's surprising though is that there's not one major building in Manhattan that was built by African Americans. Not even in Harlem. I've got one site under contract and I'm getting ready to acquire another one. It'll be downtown overlooking the water, an iconic building.

My grandfather was a hotel doorman at the Wardman Park Marriott for forty-one years. He would have been proud of me because many years later, I built and own a Marriott Hotel in that same city! I'm self-made in terms of creating wealth, but the tools that I have utilized and deployed in business come from a long family history of supporting and believing in one another and loyalty, integrity and commitment. What always puzzles me is that I'll hear, from time to time, other people who are self-made say, "I came from nothing." I generally will politely correct people. I come from a strong family legacy of character, integrity, vision, loyalty and those fundamental things as a human being that gave me the resources that are far greater than money.

The same could be said about Reginald Lewis. I've met his mother several times and that's a more valuable asset than leaving a child with money. I was honored with the Reginald F. Lewis Enterpreneural Award, which underscored for me the importance in life of growth and change. At the same time we need to inspire additional wealth creation, especially to rebalance the tremendous disparity. If you look at Hispanics, African Americans and other minorities, the opportunity to create wealth is very important because we're in a capitalistic society. I don't care how much discussion there is about taxes and so forth, that's not gonna change. So in order to have great opportunity in this country, it does require financial opportunity and resources.

My goal was to make enough money to provide financial security for my family, but it was also to have an impact on society and to create opportunities for those who didn't have it. If you work just for money, you lose focus and get bored, because at a certain point you have enough money. I go to speak to kids in high school and college to really inspire them and get them to think about entrepreneurship. The time to do that is in high school. That's when they're much more receptive to understanding it. I've endowed a program at the Hospitality High School in Washington, D.C. They have an entrepreneurial curriculum that teaches young people about owning restaurants and hotels, any kind of hotel-related business.

In my book, *The Peebles Principles,* I make several points, and some of them can apply to Reginald Lewis. For example, "If the key doesn't fit, change the lock." He had to go and regroup and find other opportunities when he went to work at a law firm and tried to become a partner. Couldn't do it that way, so he started his own law firm. It's basically creating your own opportunities and not taking "No" for an answer. Another is to "Be the last man standing." No quitting when it looks dim, figuring out a way out to win, being able to stay standing. If you can do that, you will be successful. If the wind is too strong, you can still hold on. Make the problems smaller, and find an effective way to overcome obstacles. And you cannot allow yourself to be a punching bag or a victim. Certainly in business you can't do that. It will save you from having to fight other battles later.

# Byron Eugene Lewis Sr.

*BYRON EUGENE LEWIS SR. is Chairman Emeritus of the UniWorld Group, Inc. Uniworld, founded in 1969, is the oldest full service multi-cultural marketing communications agency in the United States. Some famous works included Burger King's "We may not be the world's No. 1 fast food place; it's just tastes that way," the movie "Shaft," Reverend Jesse Jackson's first presidential campaign, and the United States Marine Corps. His television productions include "America's Black Journal."*

When I started I had never worked in an advertising agency and I had no formal business or financial background. With $250,000 from two venture capitalists, we survived for about seven years. We then got a Small Business Administration loan to continue, but the bank agreed to give us only about seventy-five percent. We were working for General Foods at the time and Lee Archer, one of the Tuskegee Airmen, was a vice president of the company. He recommended us to a Minority Enterprise Small Business Investment Company (MESBIC) for funding and that's where I met Reginald Lewis.

Reginald's company was a pioneer in helping corporations work with minority companies and he was considered the person who really helped black capital development. MESBICs resulted from affirmative action which, in the late sixties and early seventies, said to major Fortune 500 corporations and communication companies, "If you get business from the federal government, you have to have a percentage of African American and female employees." We got the MESBIC loan despite our very weak financial position and how we managed our original investment. Lee told me what influenced Reggie was that he admired my high energy level, ethical standards, work habits, and courage to work through challenges and disappointments. He said they were the best indications of our ability to repay the loan and sustain ourselves on an ongoing basis.

Advertising agencies need media to place ads and commercials. We work with major clients who want to reach minority consumers. We pay the media and vendors. And we have to be accountable to our clients based on how the money was spent and what return we received. You have to understand that back then the industry was not really supportive of black consumerism. *Ebony* magazine was the only place for ads targeting black people in any national medium. *Black Enterprise* followed, then *Essence* and *Soul Train*. Even though we were struggling, we were held to the same standards as the mainstream agencies. Reggie helped companies like us meet the standards, vouched for us, and gave a lot of common sense advice and counsel. We were venturing into uncharted waters. He was an inspiration to us struggling black business people.

Uniworld was hired to work as a black-owned company. It was not necessarily with the thought that we would be as important as I think we've grown to be, but it was sort of what conservative white people call an entitlement. I would generalize and say that they consider anything that black people did was just because they were black, disadvantaged and they were being given handouts. But the truth is, white privilege is just the same thing. They hire their relatives, people with the same backgrounds.

I named the company UniWorld because I used to be a social worker and was in downtown Manhattan in the late late fifties and early sixties in an area where all of the ethnic groups first established themselves. I said, "I think I'll call it UniWorld," because nobody knew who I was. It's just a blessing and divine intervention.

Lori-Lane, which owns a real estate company in Brooklyn, acquired my fifty-one percent in Uniworld upon my retirement. The owners' daughter, Monique Nelson, had worked for Motorola in the U.S. and internationally. She became our senior vice president of brand integration and now heads our company. She is a very beautiful, talented and driven young woman. For her age, what she's doing is a remarkable challenge, but she has the background and we've got the marketplace. The total population of African Americans, Hispanics and Asians in this country is over 110 million people, almost $3 trillion in annual income. I will be attached to UniWorld for the next couple of years. I still have a great belief in the company's destiny, and think the next plateau is really global.

We are now associated with WPP plc, the world's largest advertising agency and marketing services group. It certainly helped our financial understanding and practices. We also work with some of the clients they had, and it's been a partnership that basically has helped us survive to this point. We're the only autonomous agency in their structure, because they own everybody else.

I remember Reggie as a sophisticated person and an out-and-out entrepreneur. My folks used to say, "Have a good job so you could get social security." There are people like Reginald Lewis who see something else, and have the capabilities and confidence to do things that they see white people doing. And that was the theme of his book, *"Why should white guys have all the fun?"* Tom Brokaw wrote a book called *The Greatest Generation*, about how people after World War II really became the foundation for a parallel growth in the United States economy, politics, etc. But he never has any mention of black people. I was lucky to come from our "great generation," people like athlete Jackie Robinson, businessman Bruce Llewellyn, and Reggie Lewis. I was around them, and perhaps that was my inspiration.

Loida Lewis is a book in her self. She mourned for a year when her husband died, then restructured Beatrice International. She is one of the few people whom I think is as well known as her husband. She's philanthropic and equally versed and involved in the black and Asian communities, the business world and the women's movement. She's a gorgeous, highly intelligent woman. I've never seen a person in public life speak so much about love, other than Michelle Obama in her address to the Democratic National Convention. Loida always introduces everything, when she speaks before audiences, with a word about her beloved husband. You don't hear anybody say that.

# Robert L. Johnson

*ROBERT L. JOHNSON is Founder and Chairman of the RLJ Companies, that includes financial services, real estate, hospitality, professional sports, film production, automotive and gaming industries; founder of Black Entertainment Television (BET) network; and the first African American billionaire.*

A guy named Herb Wilkins, a long-term friend of mine, said, "Bob, you gotta meet this guy Reginald Lewis. He is dealing with all the top banking guys, all the investment houses, and he is as tough as nails, and you need to be like him, to be doing what he's doing." I said, "Gee, I've heard of him but never met him." The first time I saw a picture of him he was on the cover of *Black Enterprise* and I said, "Oh, the guy who's on *Black Enterprise*?" He said, "Yes."

That's how I got a chance to meet him. I was going just with the hope that he'd sprinkle some of his pixie dust on me and he would say, "Oh yeah Bob, I heard about you, what you're trying to do in cable. I'd like to maybe invest a couple of dollars with you," and then I'd be able to go around and say, "Hey, look, I got Reginald Lewis invested with me and look at me." I was just there to be sort of blessed with his interest. I was excited about meeting him. We talked, and he said, "You know, one day we're gonna do business, just not now." He made no bones about saying what was on his mind. If he had any hidden fears, he kept them completely under wraps, both to his inner circle and potential competitors.

I think we were both confident in our own belief in self and belief that we could achieve anything we set out to do. We probably also had a certain level of leadership skills and the charisma that sort of caused people to want to be a part of your inner circle and follow you in a deal. In our own way we both wanted to— to use the old Star Trek language—go to places no one has ever gone before, until I think he wanted to be a player at a level where no one else was at the time, not even John Johnson of *Ebony.* In particular, he wanted the business world to know he was going places. In my own way I wanted to be a first in a lot of areas and that was sort of what was driving me and I think in a way that idea of being first and visible as a first was sort of what drove Reggie.

Reginald Lewis viewed himself as a very competent, smart, urbane, sophisticated dealmaker. I don't think he necessarily wrapped himself around the idea of "I'm creating a racial statement." He was creating a Reginald Lewis Statement. He was saying, "I can play the game the same way the other guys play it and I can enjoy all the trappings of being successful in that game that the other guys do and I'm not going to be bashful about showing it off." Some people might call him cocky, but he had the right to be, because he didn't see himself in any way different than anybody else who has the smarts to play at the money manipulation game. I can remember Reggie had an office that said, "I'm not trying to hide my success." When I visited him he had some great French antiques and Persian rugs on the floor. He was just that kind of guy. His whole demeanor of flying around on private jets as soon as he could, and drinking champagne, and dressing like he was from Saville Row, it was his style. Being a billionaire was just sort of like a grade in school, you reach a level and they mark it that that's what you've done, but it's not something that defines you. It's just an example of what you can achieve if given the opportunity, if you put your intellect, a concerted effort, a level of commitment and your work ethic to make it happen. When Reg started out, there was one deal that almost bankrupted him. But it didn't stop him. He just kept going. And that's one of the things that I admired about him. You gotta believe every challenge has a solution and draw on all your resources to implement that solution. You never lose confidence in yourself that you can make it work.

The thing about Reggie that I always knew is that he was never intimidated. It wasn't like he was ever going to let—no matter who it was he was dealing with, whether they were the large money center banks or investment bankers, or junk bond guys—he wasn't gonna be intimidated. He knew numbers well. He knew how to strike a deal, how to structure deals in a tax-efficient way and how to leverage all the different vehicles of debt, equity, and mezzanine debt. He knew all the tools of the trade as well as anybody else. That's what made him so formidable. That also made him understand that you've gotta be arrogant with some of this, because a lot of it was as much style as it was financial substance. Part of doing the deals was not just because you had a lot of money, it was the art of negotiating the deals.

# Helene D. Gayle

*DR. HELENE D. GAYLE is President and CEO of CARE USA, a humanitarian aid organization fighting global poverty in nearly eighty-seven countries. Previously she worked primarily on HIV/AIDS with the Centers for Disease Control, then directed programs on HIV/AIDS and other global health issues at the Bill & Melinda Gates Foundation.*

I read about Reginald Lewis and was so impressed and proud of how bold and incredibly courageous he was and his willingness to take on tough battles. He clearly faced a lot of challenges with corporate America and upset a lot of the status quo. He was a force, a real beacon in so many ways and an unabashed advocate for black business. It seemed like he came from nowhere, but as you read more about him and his background, he had a really strong family that gave him a good grounding, a sense of himself, a community, self-confidence, and the ability to succeed. They taught him about entrepreneurship early on as a child, and encouraged him to be the best he could be. He also had a wife who was incredibly supportive. I sense she was a real strong factor standing by him and was a large part of his grounding. It was not surprising, what he did. He was just a true pioneer. He was kind of "Wow!"

You look at Reginald Lewis and others and you say, "Gee whiz, if he could do it with all the challenges that he faced, that no one who looked like him had done before, then I can do it." At times when you face discouragement and challenges, it's having those people around you who don't always tell you what you want to know, but do support you and make sure that you continue to believe in yourself. I have broken new ground, being an African American and a woman, in many of the things that I've done. There are always going to be challenges when you're trying to make a difference. You just keep putting one foot in front of the next and making sure you have the supportive networks.

Reginald Lewis was a pioneer in philanthropy. For so many African Americans, who were the first in their family to have considerable wealth, there hasn't always been the inclination to be as philanthropic as he was. He formed a family foundation in 1987. During his life he gave $1 million to Howard University that was unsolicited, $3 million to Harvard Law School and other donations. All in all, he gave $10 million that he knew would have a long-term impact. It would have been easy to just say, "This is mine and my family's," but he was a visionary in many ways and saw that part of one's responsibility is the saying, "To whom much is given, much is expected."

We've got all of these incredibly wealthy entertainers and athletes who are becoming a group of considerable wealthy African Americans. They could probably do more philanthropically, represented by the amount of wealth we have, that is sustainable and able to create change. The tradition of broader philanthropy is starting, but there's still a ways to go. Sheila Johnson and Oprah Winfrey have been incredibly philanthropic. It's easy to form a small foundation and do small acts of charity. But are we supporting our institutions that have a long-term history and will continue, that are sustainable, not just the things that make you feel good for the moment? The church is one way in which everyday African Americans have been giving for a long time to civic and other organizations. Nonprofit organizations need to diversify their leadership to attract more giving.

I look at the trend of billionaire philanthropy. Ted Turner started out by giving a billion dollars to the United Nations and the U.N. Foundation. That started Bill Gates, Warren Buffett, and others. Having people within a community to show that kind of example really does help. Reginald Lewis was a forerunner. Unfortunately, he's not still around to be able to talk about his philanthropy and get the word out. Highlighting what he did is an important part of helping to solidify that trend in the African American community. It happens by people seeing examples.

# Raymond J. McGuire

*RAYMOND J. McGUIRE is Head of Citigroup's Global Banking, which includes its Corporate and Investment Banking divisions. Past positions include Global Co-Head of Mergers & Acquisitions at Morgan Stanley and Managing Director in the Mergers & Acquisitions Group of Merrill Lynch & Co., Inc. McGuire has also been associated with Wasserstein Perella & Co., Inc., and The First Boston Corporation. But he started his career as a lawyer, inspired when he was growing up by "Perry Mason."*

For me, it was Reginald Lewis's example, rather than direct personal influence. I did not know him as intimately as others, but I certainly knew of him. He operated at a level that was peer to peer with the leaders in the business community. He was as insightful and sophisticated as any of them. At the time that Reg was able to consummate the transaction, it was a frontier in modern-day mergers and acquisitions. It was in the eighties and early nineties, and most of the techniques, the law, the structures that govern how we practice today were created back when he was at the height of his career. His record of accomplishment is unassailable. He competed at the highest levels and he did it successfully.

History will report on things that he could have done differently. But history will also report that this man was as accomplished as any in his field. He represented the best in the class. He was distinguished because he was African American. There were so few competing in that forum. I don't think I was surprised by his success. I was proud. It was a natural evolution. If he were alive today, I think he would serve as a primary example to anyone about the results of hard work, dedication and commitment to excellence.

I grew up wanting to be either a great litigator, like Perry Mason or a doctor like Ben Casey. Those were the television characters I was heavily influenced by, which is why I applied to law school. These characters both had significant influences, one in the courtroom and the other as a physician. They were eager to help, were winners and always victorious. That's what guided me.

The path from either medicine or law to financial services was happenstance. I learned about financial services while having a hot dog at the pastry restaurant in Harvard Square. There was a business school classmate of mine who had seen me in class and thought I would be good at the financial services business. There were 450 to 500 classmates who interviewed for two summer positions and I got one of the two.

Epictetus, the great philosopher, says, "Only the educated are free." So I wanted to get as much education as I could. I applied to law school and business school and got into both Harvard Law School and Harvard Business School after Harvard College. During the second year of graduate school, which is the second year of a joint program, I tried out financial services and liked it. Twenty-some odd years later, I think it turned out all right. It's a constant challenge to your mind and talents. Reginald was on the principal side of the business. I've been able to advise on $500 billion worth of transactions.

There are people I can point to on whose shoulders I stand: Joe Perella, Bruce Wasserstein, Frank Thomas, Vernon Jordan and Gordon Davis.

I tell people my biggest achievement is a lot of prayer and hard work. I grew up in the Church of God in Christ (COGIC), a Pentecostal Holiness Christian denomination. I've been blessed and fortunate. If that translates into confidence, that's because I've been given certain gifts for which I am eternally grateful.

Mine is a walk of faith, always has been and always will be. And faith always gets tested. When you come up the rough side of the mountain, you always look forward and you look up and keep focused on true north.

# Philip G. Freelon

*PHILIP G. FREELON, Founder and President of The Freelon Group, led the design team for the Reginald F. Lewis Museum of Maryland African American History and Culture and was the architect of record for the Smithsonian Institution National Museum of African American History and Culture, opening on the National Mall in Washington, D.C., in 2015.*

I thought his book had an interesting title, *"Why should white guys have all the fun?"* It was noteworthy and humorous. At the same time, it had poignancy to it. In that arena you just didn't see African Americans dealing at that level and so I would imagine that succeeding at that level and achieving that kind of success would be fun.

With the Reginald F. Lewis Museum in Baltimore, we felt it should help convey the story of Maryland African Americans, not just be a beautiful building in which exhibits would be inserted. The Maryland flag, red, yellow, black and white, is unique to the state. African Americans in Maryland represent a dichotomy. There's the struggle, strife and challenges we all know about. There's also the vibrancy and joy of our culture that's part of the larger American experience. The red wall is an intervention. It could be perceived as an abrupt way of introducing the entry point into the building. But it's also vibrant, representing vitality and free expression. So we're expressing the joy and the pain.

In the architectural field, budget and schedule are always an issue, getting the most for the dollars that are available for construction and design. Then you have to satisfy a board of thirty of forty people, the director, major donors, the constraints of working in an urban environment such as zoning regulations and building codes. One of the challenges of an urban site is that it had a small footprint, so we had to go vertically, while in a museum lots of things want to be on the main floor. But we look at these constraints as opportunities for creative solutions. In architecture, you have to stop designing at some point and get it built and move forward. There's always room for improvement. I'm happy with the building. There are lessons learned that we carry forward to other projects.

With our designs, we hope they will inspire a visitor to learn more about the building and exhibits. Approach it with an open mind and inquisitive nature. Why are these colors used? Why are the stairs designed that way? How does the light come down to the building? We want to make the patron work a little bit on a spiritual and intellectual level and not be quite so literal.

When we were selected for the National Museum of African American History and Culture on the National Mall, it was the result of an international competition: I.M. Pei, Norman Foster, Diller Scofidio, Moshe Sofdie, and Antoine Predock. The Smithsonian agreed that we had a very strong team and very compelling design. The stakes were high, but I felt like I was born to this. Our firm had been tracking this project for many years. It was a deliberate, thoughtful approach to acquiring the commission and executing it. You don't go into something like this thinking, well, it's hopeless. It was by no means slam-dunk, but this is something that I was prepared for, that my firm and others on our team put our best effort into it and continue to do so.

A key theme of the building is faith, hope and resilience. It goes back to listening. What's the vision and mission of the institution? As architects, it's not about what we want as individuals. We interpret the needs of the users and clients and listen and respond to that.

I have a passion for architecture. I hadn't met any architects until I got to college. I felt that architecture might be something that would be interesting and it happened to be a perfect fit for my interests and skill set. Black architects currently represent about two percent of the licensed architects in the U.S., and the profession is very small—about 120,000 licensed architects in the country. I'm hoping to see more African American architects. When the teachers call, I answer, "Yes, we'll send someone over to Career Day at your high school or junior high to talk about it." The visibility piece is something we, who are in the profession, can work on.

# James D. White

*JAMES D. WHITE is Chairman, President and CEO of Jamba Juice Company, which, with more than 750 locations in the United States, is a restaurant retailer of beverage and food offerings, including fruit smoothies and juices, as well as teas, oatmeal, yogurt and baked goods.*

Reginald Lewis would be a great coach to leaders in a wide range of industries. I'd be hopeful that I'd have a chance to actually know him if he were alive. I assume that he would have built significantly on his legacy from TLC Beatrice. What would have made him a great coach was just being available to share the wisdom and learning accumulated over many, many years to make himself available as what I would describe as a servant-leader. None of us get here on our own and I think the legacy, at least for me, that I would like to be able to leave is that I left the place a little bit better then when I got there, whether it's the company or lives I touch.

Reginald Lewis inspired me as a young executive coming up in my career. I had a copy of the portrait from his book in my office at Ralston Purina Company during my time there, as a daily reminder. It still sits in my home office today. He laid out a road map of what was possible and could be achieved at the very highest levels of business. There was a face and a person who looked like me.

Reading and re-reading his book, just about the sheer force of will and the tenacity that he applied to accomplish the many things that he did across his career—it's about having a big ambition, making big bets. I don't think I'll face a tougher challenge than I did when I took the helm at Jamba. I thought it was a great brand, but the company had been mismanaged. I never had a question of whether I would turn the company around or not and we did. But there's an internal compass as well that is aimed at getting the job done. Doing work that really matters. I run a company that is focused on inspiring and simplifying healthy living.

Looking ahead, more African Americans will take the helm of companies as CEOs. More importantly, you'll see more owners like Reginald Lewis. We haven't made as much progress around ownership of multimillion-dollar businesses as I would have hoped for. If he were still alive, I assume he would have a multibillion-dollar checking portfolio of businesses. I'd love to see more access to capital for African American entrepreneurs. I believe he would be a catalyst for that. I am very optimistic that we will continue to see progress in African Americans building and owning significant companies in the great spirit of Reginald Lewis.

# Shawn Baldwin

*SHAWN BALDWIN is Founder, President, and CEO of Capital Management Group (CMG), an investment advisory firm that since 2002 has participated in seventy-five capital market transactions worth more than $68 billion. Baldwin, who always says his business idol is Reginald F. Lewis, is the second African American to become a member of the Chicago Stock Exchange and has two seats on the Exchange.*

I can see myself surpassing Reginald Lewis, to the extent that I get a lot longer time. As far as what he did in that timeframe, in terms of innovation and everything else, no one's going to surpass him, because I wouldn't even think this was possible. To the extent that I'm granted life and I have time, I and other people will go beyond what he's done, but it's because that key step was put in place. He helped us imagine and envision that we could go and acquire million-dollar businesses, and not be from some families, or have $100 million in the bank. That's what I see for myself and for legions of other people, because pretty much everybody in my generation has his book as a Bible. We all like, live and die by it. Lewis is the guy.

I like to call him the progenitor. He innovated finance for black people. You don't have a lot of African Americans in financial services, but there are more now and it continues to expand. You look at the seventy-five most powerful blacks on Wall Street. Every single one of them has read, *"Why should white guys have all the fun?"* Now I realize seventy-five are not a lot of people, but it's not the same seventy-five anymore. There are other people coming in, all of whom have been affected by this book. It is one of their inspirations for going off to Wall Street or becoming entrepreneurs. They believe it can be done and that we didn't have to start from the ground up and build it. We could acquire. That was a very big jump. I actually get extra copies of his book and hand it out to people who I think will get value from it.

Reg sought out Mike Milken before he needed him because he was the guy who mastered fixed-income transactions and high-yield debt and you had to go to him. Milken received death threats for helping him. Reg studied what people did, how the transactions work, read all the memoranda and prospectuses and he replicated the successful ones and improved upon them. He got it. He was a little too sharp and that's a highly competitive space. At that time, guys figured out that he could do stuff on his own and go beyond them. He was the apprentice who could go beyond his mentors. Having all that laid out in his book—which reads as a wonderful story—was also a blueprint that is inspiring to so many people.

I feel so much has been done to squelch his legacy. This is why it was so important to have the Reginald Lewis Museum and other legacies, like the Harvard International Law Center, and even a movie, because it's great to translate that story to the general populace and keep it alive. And to the extent that you have Internet technology, people can also research and find out about his life, because he was that kind of figure. As excited as people got about President Obama, here's a guy who actually comes from a very challenging place and really made his mark on the world. He definitely outlined excellence and how you can overcome any obstacles and be a superstar success in this country.

Most guys who are on the Street tend to have either lots of ego, lots of insecurity, or a nasty combination of the two. Reg was the boss and in charge and that was very clear. He directed the traffic, no question. Those guys routinely slap each other around, have spats and disputes and then later on make up. Look at hedge fund manager Phil Falcone and his fights with Carl Icahn over the telecommunications company, LightSquared. I think it's generally accepted that it's nothing personal. It is just business and it can get rough. It's hard to get in and the margin for error is so small. Once you start fighting, everything becomes a fight, one that you have to win.

# Fay Ann Lee

*FAY ANN LEE graduated from the Wharton School of Business and, despite offers from investment banks, she decided to follow her passion to be an actress and singer. Lee first appeared on Broadway in "Miss Saigon," but quickly learned that there were few opportunities for Asian Americans in the theater. So she wrote, produced, and directed "Falling for Grace," the story of an Asian American woman working on Wall Street and living in Chinatown who tries to break into New York high society. The essence of the play, she says, is about self-esteem "and to know that who you are is truly good enough."*

Reginald Lewis knew how to play the game with the establishment. With *"Falling for Grace"*, they said "Can't you change it to be for Hispanics? Because that's much more marketable." I saw their point, but I thought, "Well, really, there are hundreds of writers, probably, writing for Jennifer Lopez." Some people in Hollywood look at me and say, "Your English is so good." It's always a shock to me. It makes me feel that being Asian American isn't American enough.

I have a new project now. I love what I wrote, but it doesn't star an Asian American and I was pretty much told, "You need to write something more commercial." Also, Asian Americans don't have a very strong network to support one another. African Americans have a much better support system. Look at Tyler Perry's movies. Hollywood didn't support him until he was able to get his movies out and prove he had a market. But in the beginning it was pretty much African Americans who would go see his movies. Asian Americans need to hone in on a good way to get the backing of our community. We really haven't figured it out exactly.

I'm not sure about the biggest mistake Reginald Lewis made, but one of the things I know is the importance of having a mentor to guide you, not to make the mistakes I did. There were lots of things that motivated me to work hard, including the fear of failure. I wanted to prove myself to my family, and to the investors who gave me the money. I cared a lot about how people saw me at face value. I would not be bold enough to ask for help because I was afraid to look bad. That was a mistake. I am hard working and capable. This is the most important thing for anyone who wants to succeed. I learned that from Reginald Lewis as well. He worked so, so hard. You don't have to have it all, but if you don't work hard, you can't make it.

In reading his book I understood how he felt in terms of his struggle to become who he was. He was fighting the system a lot, and it's how I feel also. I did think at some point I was playing in a world I didn't belong in. For Reginald Lewis it was the same thing. It is a certain establishment out there that runs my industry and that ran his. Every industry has its club and, unless you're invited to belong to it, you're not going to be able to break through easily. I still feel like an outsider, even after making my first film. If I wrote a film that made $150 million, then I'd be an insider. My industry is about money.

Reginald had so much courage to stand up for himself and that is a really valuable lesson. I need to have the courage to seek help, to call up some of these important people and say to them, "I need your support for my second movie. This is something that can make you money." Hollywood is still run by white guys, so just like Reginald Lewis, I need to set up my own rules, but I also need to work extra hard to earn their respect. The moxie that Reginald Lewis had, I'm still trying to find. You just have to do it. You can't sit there and wish that someone could do it for you. And if I'm not getting the establishment, the white guys, to help me, then I need to figure out a way to do this, to get it done myself.

# Eugene A. Profit

*EUGENE PROFIT is Founder and President of Profit Investment Management, LLC, with more than $2 billion in assets. He says, "We started small and grew by most of the time outperforming the market." Profit is also a former American football cornerback for the New England Patriots and Washington Redskins.*

Reginald F. Lewis has had a significant influence on my life. Reading his book, and many articles about him, helped me realize the importance of expanding your reach and making sure you have options as you're navigating through life. Similar to Reggie, I didn't grow up with a silver spoon in my mouth and realized early on the importance of hard work and doing your best.

Although a talented football player and track athlete, I wanted to be a good student and was afforded the opportunity to attend Yale University. By senior year, I was pretty sure that I was going to play pro football. But I made sure to leave Yale with two papers—my football contract and my B.A. degree in economics. I knew the average life of a pro football player is short lived and that, by earning my degree, I was setting myself up to have options in the future.

I read that Reggie also loved football and I, like he, prepared myself for a life after football. Even before Reggie was injured he had started to shift his focus and put that competitive passion and talent into the area of business. Similarly, while I was playing football, I started researching owning my own restaurant. When a hamstring injury in 1989 ended my football career, I didn't miss a beat and started a full-service bakery, making everything from donuts to wedding cakes.

Although it was enjoyable owning a bakery and being an entrepreneur, I missed intellectual stimulation. So I took advantage of another option available to me—I put my economics degree to use and started working in financial services. My first experience in this arena was as a financial advisor for Legg Mason. But I left that to go back to my entrepreneurial roots and started my own investment advisory firm. I founded our company with $100,000 in 1996 and we are now at a couple billion dollars in assets under management. Most of our companies are large U.S. companies. If your process is sound, you kinda stick to your knitting.

As a result of reading *"Why should white guys have all the fun?"* I also learned the importance of networking and associating yourself with people who have similar interests. One of Reggie's strongest relationships was with Mike Milken. In fact Reggie probably put himself in a position where Mike Milken sought him out. I feel that networking is extremely important and is one of the keys to my success.

Pro athletes, in my opinion, are increasingly learning the importance of networking. After receiving the Reginald F. Lewis Entrepreneurial Award in 2011, I started receiving calls from NFL players expressing their interest in business. When I talk to some of these players I say, "You might make the Hall of Fame but, even if you do, your football life is going to wrap up by the time you're thirty-five. Hopefully you're going to live another thirty-five or more years, so you want to have something else that you are just as passionate about. Having other options will let you take advantage of your competiveness for the rest of your life."

In regard to the enormous salary that football players and most other professional athletes make, I tell them "It's okay for you not to know how to best invest your money. But ask the question, "How do I preserve and grow my assets?" Then seek the advice of professionals. There are people in the know who will help you by providing counsel, manage your assets and help you invest in areas that enable you meet your financial goals.

Some individuals are short sighted when it comes to managing their own financial portfolio. They look for returns in two to three months, sometimes even in two to three days. My philosophy is similar to Warren Buffet's—value investing that yields results over a five years or more window.

One thing that came through in Reggie's life is that he tried to show the possibilities for African American businessesmen to lead certain lifestyles; for having the finer things in life like a house in the Hamptons, the parties, the country club—things that give you access to certain people and deal-making. That may be the next phase where African-American businessmen really have to get to. Bob Johnson is begininng to show that a little bit.

Another lesson I learned from Reggie is to keep moving forward. Everyone has setbacks in life—Reggie had them and I certainly have had my fair share. As a money manager, I've had both good and bad performance periods. I've been doing this long enough that I know there are ebbs and flows in the market cycle. Through all of these ups and downs, it is important to maintain your convictions and to keep your head up.

Reginald F. Lewis is one of my heroes, a hero in our community, and I am delighted that Loida is ensuring that his legacy continues.

# Mignon Espy-Edwards

*MIGNON ESPY-EDWARDS has a BA in economics from Spellman College. Mignon then went to work for the Small Business Administration Center. She gained executive sales and marketing experience at Universal Music Group and Warner Music Group and then struck out on her own as head of Grey Science, a public affairs-marketing firm.*

The title, *"Why should white guys have all the fun?"* was aggressive enough to make me want to pick the book up because I knew I was about to enter a dog-eat-dog business world. I was fascinated to read about somebody who really wasn't getting a lot of press out there at the time, except in the business press.

After college I worked for the Small Business Development Center. Later I went into the music business, working for the Island Def Jam Music Group, among others. At Def Jam, my roster included Jay Z, Bon Jovi, Kayne West, Lionel Ritchie and Mariah Carey. I was the stuff that blood and guts are made of. My old boss used to say the radio stations were playing mostly all R&B and no hip hop and now the world is playing all hip hop and a little bit less R&B every day. Russell Simmons and others were amazing teachers to me. They showed me how to kick doors if people cracked them open.

I sold the first rap records to Walmart. You can imagine me, getting on a plane going to Bentonville, and nobody looks like me. I'm trying to explain how rap is going to do really well, saying people should have access to buy goods and services in their small towns. We went back to the lab, watered down the lyrics, took out the curse words, the bad stuff, and brought it back. Walmart now has great rap business.

I know there was criticism of violence and attitude toward women with rap records. The little entrepreneur in me overlooked that and saw this more as an exercise of empowerment and wealth for those artists. They had literally come out of the projects, came and sat in my office every day and said, "Teach me about sales."

I showed them how they could make a product, take it to market, sell it and what that meant in the grand scheme of things in terms of entertainment—who their peers were, their competitors, and how we could work together and figure out ways to outdo the competition. The more exposure they got, the less damaging were the lyrics. Jay-Z doesn't rap about bitches anymore. He's talking about life experiences. I'm okay with him rapping about planes, cars and money.

I figured if I could structure and do strategy for people to make millions of dollars, I could do it for myself. I had gotten to a point where people were contacting me. My Rolodex, with more than 6,000 contacts, was just hot. When people are bringing you deals and you don't have any current infrastructure to vet them and source them, it's time for a change. Record companies weren't making all the money they were accustomed to and they're challenging and kicking me in the butt to figure out how I am going to make up for the lost income. And when you bring them opportunities and they pass on them, then go across the street to another company and make millions, you start to realize, why should white guys have all the fun? Hey, white guys don't have all the answers either. You know if you got the butter, the milk and make the cake for yourself, what else do you need?

After leaving the music business and opening up my own business, I was upset that Reginald Lewis's legacy needed to be forwarded from a business end. I was talking with one of my clients, ING, and suggested that the bank put aside $50,000 for the Reginald F. Lewis Foundation's endowment. The bank is also giving $200,000 to the National Urban League Entrepreneur Centers in their satellite offices around the country for The Reginald F. Lewis Fellows Program. It will be similar to what the Small Business Development Center does—teach people the skills they need to run businesses. Some of them have never started a business, others have. They'll learn how to weather tough times, how to make sure they're looking toward the future and have a business where people want to work for you.

I think Reginald had a bigger plan in life. It wasn't so much about the art of the deal. He was here to make life a better place, to show us that there are so many ways to live the dream and provide opportunity. If he had to be out there to fight the battle, to show the inequality, the prejudice, to go out and slay those dragons, just to prove the point, then he was going to do it. He would have been passionate to have brothers and sisters learning how to be entrepreneurs. Just understanding how there's more in the deal than just the money. There's a negotiation feeling behind it, finding out where the other side is coming from, and sometimes your opponent can end up just being a real friend. You can respectfully disagree and understand each other's position and what kind of skin they have in the game. Better to know exactly what the other person wants before you get there.

# L. Londell McMillan

*L. LONDELL MCMILLAN, ESQ. is a Partner at Meister, Seelig & Fein, LLP and Chairman of The NorthStar Group, which publishes* Jones Magazine *and* The Source. *As an entertainment lawyer, his clients have included Prince, Lil' Kim, Stevie Wonder, Chaka Khan, Spike Lee, and Michael Jackson.*

Mr. Lewis told me to go into corporate finance, that it was the new civil rights imperative of my generation. And that's what I did. There are so many parallels between Reginald Lewis's life and mine. I had my own law firm. He had his own law firm. I drive my staff nuts. He drove his staff nuts. They think I'm very demanding and that I can be pushy. Reginald Lewis was very pushy. He was also driven and didn't see limitations. I don't see limitations. He always knew he was an African American, but did not let that limit his trajectory.

Reginald focused more on capital markets after he left the law. I have focused more on entertainment. But as I transition into a more scalable and larger platform, I will expand and look at bigger assets beyond entertainment and media that I can buy, sell and turn around by strategically partnering with others and seeking financing to be able to make deals. At the end of the day you need capital to invest and acquire assets and that has always been challenging for African Americans.

Those who are able to put together the relationship, the vehicles and the platforms to obtain capital are able to play the game. Mr. Lewis said, "Why should white guys have all the fun?" because they're often the ones with access. It's always their capital, institutional capital, private equity, hedge funds and resources that are made available for them to take risks. And we all know that often we're denied the opportunity to succeed. He truly was the Jackie Robinson of corporate finance. His story was not only one of brilliance, but also of his ability to put together a network that provided him access to capital so that he could play the game. But I don't think we've developed further from those days some twenty or thirty years ago.

He had people who were vested in what he wanted to do and wanted to see him succeed. He wasn't successful the first, second, or third time. But he was brilliant, stuck with it, and never lost faith. If you don't see victory coming, "keep going, no matter what" because the alternative is absolute failure.

Receiving the Reginald F. Lewis Entrepreneurial Award was very inspirational, an honor that I will never forget. It gave me tremendous insight, just being around all the people who knew him. I was very proud that people recognized my work and would mention my name in the same breath as his. I don't think there have been many people who've played the entertainment and media law game the way I have. Mr. Lewis was involved in a different game, international finance, and that is far more difficult in some respects.

It's easier on some levels to be a global player, but not necessarily in America, because those barriers still exist for African Americans. But with the Internet and people being much more in tune with African

American culture, from the Middle East to Europe and Africa, the opportunities are greater for global players.

I represent businesses and companies in a different way than I do music and film celebrities and pop stars. In many respects, being so attached to these very high-profile individuals is very demanding. For example, the Michael Jackson case, with respect to Mrs. Jackson, his children and Debbie Row, was just extraordinarily difficult and challenging to deal with. I have been so consumed by my clients and it has prevented me from moving on in my career, the way Mr. Lewis moved on to his next phase with his law firm and his career. I'm in that transition period.

Pop and celebrity culture is America's royalty, and those associated with them are exposed more in the public eye. When I decide to take a case, it depends on whether I believe I can offer the personal service to the client and if the client has a legitimate chance of achieving their goals and objectives. Sometimes it's not always about winning the case, but about negotiating a more fair and equitable position.

My law career has given me much more pleasure than my publishing career. I believe in bringing goals, responsibility and integrity to use in hip hop culture, and that's been missing. When I started my career, I was very inspired by hip hop in a positive way and I want to bring that kind of direction and mandate to our magazine, *The Source*. Under my leadership, it is a very pro-social, positive use of a cultural publication and digital offering. Stories like Mr. Lewis's allow me to be in the midst of a hip hop culture and stay focused. I don't get distracted because I've seen what success really looks like, what multi-billion-dollar players really look like. They look like Reginald Lewis.

*PHOTO CREDIT: Bobby Friedel*

# Elinor Ruth Tatum

*ELINOR RUTH TATUM is Publisher and Editor in Chief of the* New York Amsterdam News, *one of the oldest African American publications in the United States.*

Reginald Lewis was a friend of my father. In the black community he was this fantastic man who was able to buy TLC Beatrice, become one of the 400 richest Americans and build a billion-dollar company. It taught us that anything is possible. I think his thought was, "If I set my mind to it, I can do it. And don't get in my way, because if I don't go around you, I'll go through you. You can't stop me."

Reginald Lewis went to Michel Milken and Drexel Burnham Lambert when he wanted to make this deal. My father also went to Michael Milken, seeking help to finance the purchase of the *Daily News* back in the 1980s. Milken was the only one out there who would. But they didn't want to sell it to a black man, basically. Michael Milken and his company were the only ones that said, "You know what, black entrepreneurs are the wave of the future, and we will support them." When they came to him with something that actually made sense, he said "Why not?" instead of "Why?" I remember my father telling me that he went to all the big finance houses in New York. At one point he went to someplace, and he was in a suit, and they said, "Deliveries are in the back." That didn't happen when he went to Milken. He sat down with my dad and said, "What do you need?"

When I was seven I wanted to be the first black Jewish female President of the United States of America. My mother is Jewish, from Czechoslovakia. My father is black. I wanted to be all *three* of them together. I told my parents and they said, "If you want to do it, do it." But then I saw what was happening in politics, and how people's lives were turned so far upside down. I didn't want to be under a microscope like that and I just said, "I don't need that." I also figured I could do a lot where I worked, with what I was doing. I asked my father why he didn't run for public office—I think he might have considered mayor—and he said he had more power where he was.

When my father named me publisher and editor-in-chief, I was twenty-seven. I said, "Are you crazy?" But I knew he wouldn't have done it unless he believed in me. It was trial by fire. I was young, female, and black. Being publisher is more challenging, because it has to do with trying to find the money. When there's something that happens in the black community, people go to the black press, because that's where they know they will find the best and most information.

When I was growing up, my sixth grade teacher, because I have dyslexia, said that I really was not going to amount to anything and that basically I'd be lucky if I got a job and did anything with my life. I ran into her twice. The first time was right after I graduated from high school and she said, "So, did you get a job, or are you going to trade school?" I said, "No, actually I'm a scholar at St. Lawrence University, thank you very much," and I walked away. Five or six years later I ran into her again and she said, "So, did you graduate from college? Were you able to get a job?" And I said, "Well, yes, I'm an editor at the *Amsterdam News*. I said, "And what are you doing?" She said, "I've retired," and I looked at her and said, "Thank God."

I had another teacher at that same school. Her name was Gloria Kagan. She didn't understand learning disabilities, but she started to figure them out because of me. She realized these kids are smart, they can really do anything, they just learn differently. When the first article about me appeared in the *New York Times*, I got a letter from her, saying "It's so good to see my kids grow up so well." She was the mother of Elena Kagan, the Supreme Court Justice.

Reginald Lewis was a very unique person. There have been some out there who have tried, but they have not come up to that same level. America is still afraid of black men in power. They have done whatever they can, in my opinion, to make sure that we can't control as much as everyone else does. When we have power and influence, we can make a change. We will have our young people being educated and going into different directions, rather than the prison system.

Look at the Fortune 500. How many black CEOs are there? People will say, with Barack Obama as President, you've gotten the highest job in the land, but the thing is that we still don't have folks who are dictating what are on the front pages of the newspapers and television news broadcasts or making corporate decisions. Until that happens, until we've got equal representation in all segments of society, we will not have parity. Nor will we be able to have more Lewises. You can see the fight that started in the fifties, or earlier. My father always used to tell me, when I would ask, "Why didn't you teach us how to fight?" he said, "Because we thought we had done it for you with the Civil Rights Movement."

*PHOTO CREDIT: TAR*

# Through the Years

Through the years, Reginald F. Lewis and his family have had a strong commitment to philanthropy. It started way back in 1968 when Lewis sent a ten-dollar contribution to Harvard Law School while working as a junior associate at Paul, Weiss, Rifkind, Wharton & Garrison. Years later he made a much more substantial donation of $3 million to Harvard Law School, which named the International Law Center after him. Lewis also contributed, unsolicited, $1 million to Howard University and to other cultural, educational and social causes.

The Reginald F. Lewis Foundation, chaired by Loida Nicolas Lewis, has carried on this family tradition of generosity. Among the institutions the Foundation supports—in addition to Harvard—are the Reginald F. Lewis Museum of Maryland African American History and Culture, The Lewis College in Sorsogon, Philippines, the Reginald F. Lewis High School of Business and Law in Baltimore, Maryland and the Virginia State University Reginald F. Lewis School of Business.

# Robert Clark

*PROFESSOR ROBERT CLARK, ESQ., the former Dean of the Harvard Law School, is a Harvard University Distinguished Service Professor and Harvard Law School Austin Wakeman Scott Professor. In 1992 Reginald F. Lewis contributed $3 million to Harvard Law School, the largest gift ever made then to the school by an individual donor. In recognition, the International Law Center was named after him, becoming the first building at an Ivy League school to be named after an African American.*

When we started talking about our backgrounds, where we grew up, his family in Maryland, he had no idea that a dean of the law school came from New Orleans and from a kind of rundown area, right on the edge. My street was one over from a black street. At that time, in the fifties, it was all segregated, but there was still a lot of interaction among people, helped by the positive role played by the Catholic Church.

We were exchanging stories and we really hit it off after that. When we got around to our fundraising campaign, and the significance of his being involved, we talked about his experience and his realization that his going to Harvard Law School had made a difference to him. You have the talent, the drive, but getting the training, the great certification and connections make all the difference. I could see he wanted to make that possible for other people. It was a kind of giving-back instinct, a feeling that "I want to do something that will help the next generation."

My impulse as a dean was, we've got a great thing here: the next generation of African American students who are really good and can get into the top law schools, we want them to come here. We need to get his name on a building. When I first asked him for a contribution, I brought up the figure $5 million. He thought I was crazy. He said something like, "You've got a lot of nerve." And I thought, "I've lost it, he's not gonna do it." I think I told him it was something to think about. I never got excited when people gave me this reaction. He wanted minority students to benefit. When I went back to my colleagues at Harvard, I told everybody about it. They were delighted, they said, "This guy is great."

The money has been used mainly for Reginald F. Lewis Fellowships that train people, primarily minorities, to become scholars in the field of international relations and business. And I think we have lived up to it. We've had so many terrific minority students. I know from looking at my own classes it's pretty high. Reginald seemed to understand where I was coming from as a dean, as a corporate law professor and as someone who cared about the business sector, internationalism, and increasing diversity. It felt good to have a key alumnus sort of on the same page.

There are some who said, "Harvard, why not donate to a black institution?" I think he understood the importance of people of different backgrounds being at the same institution. For Reg, interaction among people of all races, ethnicities, and backgrounds was pretty important. He saw the significance of the Harvard brand. He wanted to make it something that would appeal to African Americans coming up. It was an incredibly important signal that he thought was valuable. Here's an African American graduate who really liked the school and supported it. We should all appreciate that.

It was like, "This is where you go if you want to be an important leader of business, or government, or the legal system." We have lots of models that sort of symbolize that, including our president, Barack Obama. Reginald Lewis's picture is right inside the Lewis Center on the first floor. You walk in, you see it right there. And it just stands out and says, "Look, this man was great, and you can be great too."

When I think about Reginald Lewis, I also think about his wife, Loida. What always struck me was what a wonderful pair they were. He just understood her. There's something about her exuberance, confidence, and good nature. He seemed to sense, "This is the person I want to be with. I'll go out and do the hard stuff, make the money and maybe she'll spend it on good causes."

www.law.harvard.edu

Reginald F. Lewis in the Harvard Law School Yearbook, 1968.

The Lewis Center at Harvard Law School.

# Rose Anonat

*DR. ROSE ANONAT is Officer in Charge at The Lewis College in Sorsogon City, Philippines. The school, established by Loida Nicolas Lewis, is in memory of her husband, Reginald F. Lewis and is a legacy of the Nicolas family to the people of Sorsogon. She was born and grew up in this province.*

Our students acquaint themselves with the life of Reginald F. Lewis by reading his autobiography, "*Why should white guys have all the fun?*" We have copies in our library and require our students to read it so that they will be inspired. He didn't come from an affluent family and he worked his way through college. We want our students to emulate him and to keep going.

Our students encounter a lot of difficulties, but nothing should deter them from getting an education and lifting themselves up. We always repeat a favorite phrase of Mr. Lewis, "Keep going no matter what."

The mission of our school is to "train minds, touch hearts, and transform lives." We have to train students in character building and academics. We also teach them moral responsibility, citizenship and civic consciousness. These are all important values that students should develop before they can become good employees and leaders in their community. Every task that they accomplish tells them that they have hope and can attain what Reginald Lewis did if they try and try and never give up.

Sorsogon is one of the most depressed provinces in the region, with an average family income of around $200 a month. Students really have to work hard. They get up early, come to school and do their tasks with determination. Education is their only hope and way out of poverty. It makes us proud to know that many of our graduates have jobs in offices and banks and others have started businesses. The education they receive here is critical to them being able to support their families.

One fourth of our students are on work-study, providing janitorial, student assistance and clerical services to the school. These students, because of their need, are not required to pay tuition.

Our drop out rate is very low. If someone plans to drop out, we ask, "What's the reason?" And they will often say, "Because nobody would support my daily expenses." For these students, we help them find a sponsor who lets them live and work in their home in exchange for assistance.

In academics and athletics, our students are getting better. In fact, last year a group of them ranked fifth in a Science and Information Technology contest, competing with universities throughout the Philippines. Our Pep Squad, Basketball Team and Choir are also winning competitions.

The Lewis College opened in 2000, and now has 1,620 students from pre-school through college. We have four main buildings and a gym.

The school is attracting students from nearby provinces, and many of them are from farming, fishing and cottage industry families. Our school has the lowest tuition cost in the entire region.

www.thelewiscollege.com

Latest addition to The Lewis College.

Students at The Lewis College.

The Lewis College campus.

# George L. Russell Jr.

*GEORGE L. RUSSELL Jr., ESQ., was the first African American to serve as Associate Judge of the Supreme Bench of Baltimore and also became Baltimore's first African American City Solicitor. Judge Russell led the effort to build the Reginald F. Lewis Museum of Maryland African American History and Culture in his hometown of Baltimore. Located two blocks east of the Inner Harbor, it is the East Coast's largest African American museum.*

Most black people don't come to museums because they are not exposed to them. Neither are poor whites. Museums used to be primarily for the wealthy and the socialites who would adopt museums all over the country. In our culture, museums were not the number one source of entertainment

I think Reginald would be proud of the museum. It's the most beautiful museum anywhere in America. It opened in 2005, has 82,000 square feet, and focuses on the histories of Maryland's African Americans and their familial and community bonds. Exhibits here explore the role African American labor played in building the state and national economy. It also fosters pride by presenting an accurate picture of contributions by African Americans to cultural life, politics, education and science.

The reaction to the museum has been amazing. When the State Legislature and Senate came up to look at it, they didn't believe we did it. You don't broadcast what you're doing and then, when it comes out, they say, "My Lord!" And the museum came in on time and under budget. The architects were the same ones who were designing the Smithsonian National Museum of African American History and Culture on the National Mall in Washington, D.C. Part of the museum is built on top of the Underground Railroad. We excavated it and had members of the Board lay gold down in the Foundation.

The museum has developed a curriculum, "An African American Journey," to be implemented statewide for grades K–12. White kids, along with blacks, can come to the museum and we have docents take them around. It is an opportunity to inculcate in young kids a sense of identity, to find out who they are, where they had been, and where they are going. It has a very active, unique and viable partnership with the Maryland State Department of Education.

If you look at the museum, success down the road will depend on the economy and the ability to sustain fundraising. The community and the government gave $31 million for the museum. The largest gift, $5 million, came from the Reginald F. Lewis Foundation. We have some money, but it's not what it should be. It's a challenge to operate, absolutely. You have to go out and bring the money in. Above all we have to integrate. We have to stop isolating ourselves from the main community. You have to bring in the broader community if you want to raise money.

In many ways we are our own worst enemy. We don't participate. We're an all black thing. Unfortunately, even when the school integration cases were decided on race, that was the case. I knew Thurgood

Marshall well. He's from Baltimore. But when he went in, they used race as the distinguishing, primary issue in *Brown v. Board of Education*. And yet, just a few days earlier, there was a case in Texas, *Hernandez v. Texas,* where Mexicans could not get on the jury because they were Mexican. They went in and got the same result, but without the specter of race as being the dividing line. Now whites like Bakke and others are saying, "Well, we've got rights too."

I have a son who's now a federal judge, and I hope that his son will become a judge also. We've got to pass it on. You haven't achieved anything unless you help somebody along and pass on your talent.

www.rflewismuseum.org

Reginald F. Lewis Museum of Maryland African American History and Culture, 2005.

PHOTO CREDIT: *FREELON/RTKL A Joint Venture / Photo: James West JWestProductions.com*

Web page of the Reginald F. Lewis Museum of Maryland African American History and Culture (www.rflewismuseum.org).

# Barney J. Wilson

*DR. BARNEY J. WILSON is Principal of the Reginald F. Lewis High School of Business and Law in Baltimore, Maryland. He has degrees in electrical engineering, math, economics, business and educational leadership. "I wanted to be in a school that was named after a black man."*

I really appreciated Reginald Lewis on a gut level. He was a strong African American male who had conviction and knew that he could fight for what he wanted. He was a leader. He knew he had that "it" factor. His style of dressing, the fact that he had a car early, that he was a quarterback on the football team. He knew that people were looking at him. Even when the odds were against him, he didn't recognize the word "no."

There really was no reason for him to get that acceptance into Harvard other than that he went there for the summer, pushed butt, put his best foot forward and showed up in the Dean's office saying, "Hey, I'm here. I'm not going anywhere. I want to stay." He had that type of attitude, that get-it-down attitude, the confidence in knowing what's good versus what's bad. I think he was born with it, but he also had some reinforcement. Certainly his mother and others in his family were very strong.

When I greet students at the door, either I'm going to greet them with a smile or a frown. If a child has to go through a metal detector and the bathrooms are locked, then that's not really saying I love you. It's saying I don't trust you. A black child going into a department store and having people follow him or her, or suspect them of doing things, doesn't feel loved. Some children in urban settings can be walking down the street from school and police officers might follow them. That doesn't feel like love. It suggests distrust, and that you are not welcome. At school we sign everything with "Lewis Loves." The students know what this means.

The word "love " is kind of invasive. It goes deep. You know when you are loved. You have an opportunity for success and you have hope, because someone cares about you.

But there's an expectation that goes along with that trust; that you're not going to violate the family. In our case, the family is the school. The students named the school after him. We're related to each other in trying to better our lot in life, and that's what Reginald Lewis did. When students don't show up, we go to their houses to get them. We go and talk to the neighbors. "When's the last time anyone's seen Lamont?" And when people realize that you really do care, they say, "Okay, we want that too. We want him to be in school." So you may hear an uncle saying, "You know, I heard you came around the house. You're looking for Lamont. This is where he is." We'll go and find him and say, "Hey, we miss you. Come back."

When I read the book about Reginald Lewis, I sensed that he was a man of love. What the school was missing was hope and love. Many students need a father figure. Children are raising themselves. We have homeless children and children who are not given clear guidance. Throughout the country, we have high suspension rates, high absentee rates, poor grades on transcripts and high failure rates. It's all related. Someone has to tell the individual child, "You are better than this." Being at the Reginald Lewis High School has taught me a lot. It's not just preparing a lesson plan and delivering it. What else is this child dealing with? I've also learned not to be as judgmental, to really put myself in the shoes of others, to understand their dynamics, all the while still expecting good results.

www.baltimorecityschools.org/419

Reginald F. Lewis High School, Business and Law.

Reginald F. Lewis High School, Business and Law—Graduation Ceremony.

# Keith Miller

*DR. KEITH MILLER is President of Virginia State University, which named its business school the Reginald F. Lewis School of Business. The school received a $1.5 million contribution from the Reginald F. Lewis Foundation, which will endow scholarships, student and faculty travel and will provide an academic achievement prize. Lewis graduated from VSU, on the Dean's List, in 1965.*

We made history in 2010, becoming the first school in the country to deliver our core curriculum in a predominantly digital format. We saw the need to do online education because of the rising cost of textbooks—for example, $300 a textbook—and the weight of carrying backpacks. We wanted to be on the leading edge of integrating technology into the learning experience. Publishers are really working hard to catch up to the demand and certain disciplines are further into having e-books available than others. There's also a mindset change that needs to happen in a department or unit. We were recently named the top business school in the country's historically black colleges and universities (HBCUs) for our commitment to innovation. It's a first step for us and, certainly, we want our business school to be recognized as one of the best in the country.

We pride ourselves on the fact that we don't have a lot of large classes. The environment at Virginia State provides a student faculty ratio of one to sixteen. Many students really need personal attention, smaller classes and the opportunity to know their faculty members.

We are a historically black college with a gravesite for more prominent Caucasians on our agriculture farm. We are working with the Daughters of the American Revolution to monitor that gravesite to ensure that it is preserved properly, advertised and marketed. In this instance you have a historically black college and the Daughters of the American Revolution, whose ancestors were dominant slave owners, now working together. It is a great partnership.

Our school was named after Reginald Lewis because of what he was able to do with his life and what he provided to the world. Hopefully, Virginia State helped cultivate some of that talent. Reginald Lewis entered VSU on a football scholarship, majoring in economics and political science. He lost his scholarship due to an injury and worked in a bowling alley and as a photographer's assistant. Before he graduated from VSU, he was given the opportunity to attend the summer session at Harvard Law School, which actually led to him being accepted at Harvard before even applying.

At VSU our focus includes the community. Experiential opportunities outside the classroom are very important. Internships, cooperative experiences, study abroad, service learning and volunteer work in the community are all important. It adds to the learning experience and builds a relationship that we would not otherwise have in the community. From the fruits and vegetables on our agriculture farms, we prepare meals for the homeless and hungry. As a civic minded individual, I visited the Richmond city jail. I wanted to get across the message that the inmates are not just a number. In many instances, they are individuals who can turn their lives around. Virginia State University is a beacon of hope.

www.vsubusiness.org

Reginald F. Lewis School of Business at Virginia State University.

In 1961, Lewis entered VSU on a football scholarship, but had to stop playing because of injuries.

PHOTO CREDIT: *Lin Hart*

# Memorable Photos

Lewis, fourth from right, in pledge line for Kappa Alpha Psi at VSU, circa 1963. Later the alumni established the Reginald F. Lewis Kappa Alpha Psi Inc. Alpha Psi Chapter Endowed Scholarship Fund.

PHOTO CREDIT: *Lin Hart*

At his Wall Street Law Firm, circa 1975.

At his Wall Street Law Firm, circa 1990.

With his brother, Jean Fugett Jr., in front of their home in West Baltimore.

Reginald and Loida with his grandparents, Samuel and Savilla Cooper, in West Baltimore, circa 1969.

With Loida and daughters Leslie and Christina
in Paris apartment, December 1988.

Chatting with his mother, Carolyn E. Fugett,
during lunch in Paris, circa 1989.

Sharing a light moment with Michael Milken at
Drexel Burnham Lambert conference in 1987.

With mayoral candidate David Dinkins at the Harvard Club,
where Lewis hosted a fundraiser for him in 1990.

Surrounded by his TLC Beatrice International managers and executives, circa 1988.

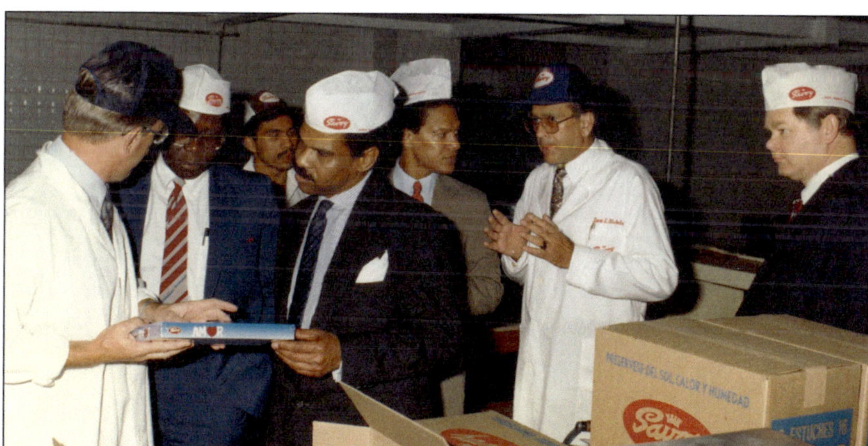

Visiting Savoy, the Venezuelan food company he sold on the same day he acquired the business.

In his custom made corporate jet with background mural, "Infinity," commissioned from internationally known African American artist Ed Clark.

Reginald F. Lewis in Paris with Eiffel Tower in background, circa 1990.

# Loida Nicolas Lewis

*In 1987, Loida Nicolas Lewis's husband, Reginald F. Lewis, a Harvard Law School graduate, bid for and won the operations of Beatrice International Foods in a $985 million leveraged buyout. It was the largest off shore leveraged buyout of its kind at that time. In 1992, Lewis was listed in* Forbes Magazine *as among the 400 wealthiest Americans. He died of brain cancer, at the age of fifty, in 1993.*

After the death of her husband, Loida served as Chair and CEO of TLC Beatrice International Holdings, Inc. food company, with operations across Europe and Asia. She won over a skeptical business community by moving quickly to increase earnings and pay down debt by selling assets, including the corporate jet and by downsizing the New York corporate staff by fifty percent. In 1995, she was on the cover of *Working Woman* magazine, featured as the "Top Businesswoman in America." After successfully running the company, she completed the sale of TLC Beatrice and its businesses, achieving a thirty-five percent internal rate of return on investment for shareholders.

Currently Loida is Chair and CEO of TLC Beatrice, LLC, a family investment firm. A lawyer by profession, admitted to practice in the Philippines and New York, she was the first Filipino woman to pass the New York Bar without attending law school in the United States.

Loida Nicolas Lewis served for ten years as General Attorney with the Immigration and Naturalization Service and co-authored the best-selling book, *How to Get a Green Card*, now in its tenth edition.

A leader in the Filipino-American community, she is one of the founders of the National Federation of Filipino American Associations (NaFFAA), an advocacy group; one of the founders of the Asian American Legal Defense & Education Fund (AALDEF); and one of the founders of U.S. Pinoys for Good Governance (USPGG), organized after the May 2010 election of Benigno Simeon Aquino III as President of the Philippines.

A well-regarded philanthropist, in 1998 Loida funded the microfinance People's Alternative Livelihood Foundation of Sorsogon Inc. (PALFSI) in her hometown. The foundation has since helped lift 20,000 families out of poverty. She succeeded her husband as Chair of the Reginald F. Lewis Foundation, which has given millions of dollars to educational and cultural institutions. Loida was recently elected to the Board of Directors of the National Catholic Reporter, an independent news organization with a global reach, and the Apollo Theater Foundation. She speaks Filipino, English, French, and Spanish.

Loida has two daughters, both *cum laude* B.A. graduates of Harvard University. Leslie is an actor and playwright, having written "Miracle in Rwanda." Christina, after a five-year stint with the *Wall Street Journal*, is a journalist and author of the best-selling *Lonely at the Top*. Loida has three grand children, Christian, Savilla, and Calvin, and two sons-in-law, Gavin Sword, a businessman, and Dan Halpern, a writer.

# Ponchitta Pierce

*PONCHITTA PIERCE is a communications expert with extensive experience in interviewing, writing, editing, research, and compiling oral histories.*

Ponchitta has been a television host and producer, a journalist, and a speechwriter. She began her career in journalism at *Ebony* magazine, where she rose to become the New York Editor and New York Bureau Chief of the magazine's parent company, Johnson Publications.

Ponchitta has worked at CBS News as a special correspondent, and at WNBC-TV in New York, where she hosted and co-produced a daily television show, *Today in New York*. She has also hosted programs for New York's PBS affiliate station, WNET.

In addition to her work in television, Ponchitta has served as a Contributing Editor for *Parade* and *McCall's* magazines, a Roving Editor for *Reader's Digest*, and has written for many national publications, including *AARP The Magazine (Modern Maturity)*, *Family Circle*, *More*, *Newsday*, and *Ladies Home Journal*. Several of her interviews appear in *My Soul Looks Back in Wonder: Voices of the Civil Rights Experience* (AARP/Sterling Publishing), a book that presents eyewitness accounts from people who had played pivotal roles in the Civil Rights Movement. Ponchitta's work also appears in the book *The Leader of the Future 2: Visions, Strategies and Practices for the New Era.*

Long active in community service, she is a member of the Board of Directors of the Foreign Policy Association; WNET; the Inner-City Scholarship Fund of the Catholic Archdiocese of New York; Housing Enterprise for the Less Privileged (H.E.L.P.); and the Cuban Artists Fund. She is also a member of the Council on Foreign Relations, The Economic Club of New York, and the Columbia-Presbyterian Health Sciences Advisory Council.

A graduate of the University of Southern California with a B.A. in journalism (*cum laude*), Ponchitta has also studied at Cambridge University in England.

PHOTO CREDIT: *Everod Nelson*

*"Keep going no matter what."*
*Reginald F. Lewis*
*December 7, 1942  January 19, 1993*

*www.reginaldflewis.com*

Made in the USA
Monee, IL
18 August 2026

60447836R00069